Generative AI for Business

How AI is Revolutionizing Productivity and Automation

James Royce Smartman

Copyright © 2024 James Royce Smartman

All rights reserved.

DEDICATION

To the visionaries, inventors, and dreamers who never stop pushing the limits of what technology is capable of.

To the companies that welcome change and use AI to turn obstacles into opportunities.

And to the innumerable people who understand that we make the future rather than waiting for it.

You should read this book.

CONTENTS

ACKNOWLEDGMENTS... 1

CHAPTER 1 1

Introduction to Generative AI and Business 1

   1.1 Defining Generative AI and Its Capabilities 1

   1.2 The Rise of Large Language Models (LLMs) 4

   1.3 Generative AI Market Growth and Future Projections 6

CHAPTER 2 10

Large Language Models (LLMs) and Their Power 10

   2.1 Understanding How LLMs Work 10

   2.2 Training and Accuracy of LLMs in Business Use Cases 13

   2.3 Future of LLMs: Sparse Expert Models and Self-Improvement 16

CHAPTER 3 21

Generative AI in Marketing and Sales 21

   3.1 AI-Generated Marketing Content: Text, Images, and Videos 21

   3.2 Customer Engagement: Conversational AI and Chatbots 25

   3.3 Predictive Sales Strategies Using AI 29

CHAPTER 4 34

Using Generative AI in Product Development and Operations 34

   4.1 AI Chatbots for Automating Customer Support 34

   4.2 Using AI to Find Production Errors and Anomalies 38

   4.3 Automating User Manuals and Product Documentation 41

CHAPTER 5 46

Engineering and IT Applications of Generative AI............................... 46

5.1 Software Development and Coding Aided by AI........................... 46

5.2 GitHub Copilot: Automating Code to Cut Down on Development Time.. 50

5.3 Using AI to Create and Complete Data Tables.............................. 53

CHAPTER 6... 58

Legal and Risk Considerations for Generative AI................................. 58

6.1 Automatically Drafting and Examining Legal Documents............ 58

6.2 Highlighting and Recapitulating Legal Developments................... 61

6.3 Using AI to Manage Patents and Contracts.................................... 63

CHAPTER 7... 67

Human Resources (HR) and Generative AI... 67

7.1 AI-Driven Interview Questions for Evaluating Candidates............ 67

7.2 Self-Serve Solutions for HR Process Automation.......................... 70

7.3 Enhancing Employee Management and Onboarding...................... 72

CHAPTER 8... 75

Using Generative AI to Optimize Employees and Utility...................... 75

8.1 Using AI-Powered Tools to Improve Employee Communication.. 75

8.2 Using AI to Create Business Presentations..................................... 77

8.3 Using AI to Combine Task Insights and Meeting Summaries........ 79

CHAPTER 9... 83

Healthcare and Synthetic Data.. 83

9.1 AI's Contribution to the Development of Synthetic Patient Data... 83

9.2 How Clinical Research Is Accelerated by Synthetic Data.............. 86

9.3 Consequences for Privacy and the Moral Application of Synthetic

Data... 88

CHAPTER 10 92

Generative AI's Role in Business 92

10.1 AI in Advertising: AI Ad Models from Google and Meta 92

10.2 Generative AI's Place in International Business Strategy 95

10.3 Generative AI's Long-Term Effect on Workforce Productivity 97

ABOUT THE AUTHOR 100

CHAPTER 1

INTRODUCTION TO GENERATIVE AI AND BUSINESS

Generative AI has emerged as one of the most revolutionary technologies in recent years, impacting different industries and revealing enormous prospects. This chapter covers the key concepts of generative AI, the technological advancements that have propelled its rise, and the ramifications for businesses globally. We will analyze the distinguishing aspects of generative AI, its capabilities, the role of Large Language Models (LLMs), and the direction of its market expansion.

1.1 Defining Generative AI and Its Capabilities

Generative AI refers to a class of artificial intelligence models meant to generate new content, whether in the form of text, images, audio, video, or even code. Unlike standard AI systems that focus on classifying, forecasting, or discovering patterns within existing data, generative AI creates new data that is coherent, creative, and contextually relevant. This characteristic shows the model's ability to simulate human-like creativity and output, making it a strong tool for multiple applications across sectors.

Types of Generative AI Models:

- **Text Generators:** Models like GPT (Generative Pre-trained Transformer) that construct human-like text depending on prompts.

- **Image Generators:** AI systems like DALL·E that can generate high-quality images from textual descriptions.

- **Audio and Music Generators:** Models that produce original audio content, including music composition and voice synthesis.

- **Code Generators:** AI tools that can write and debug software code, boosting the efficiency of engineers.

The essential power of generative AI rests in its capacity to learn from massive volumes of data and create content that follows the patterns and rules buried within that data. This gives doors to applications like:

- **Content Creation:** Automated development of articles, reports, and marketing material.

- **Product Design:** Designing new items, from fashion to industrial components, through AI-driven innovation.

- **Personalization:** Customizing experiences, such as suggestions or chat conversations, at an individual level with a thorough awareness of context and preferences.

- **Automation of Repetitive Tasks:** Generative AI may perform repetitive and mundane activities, like generating reports, thereby freeing up human resources for more strategic work.

1.2 The Rise of Large Language Models (LLMs)

Large Language Models (LLMs) offer a huge leap forward in generative AI. These models are trained on vast datasets and are capable of interpreting and creating human language with astonishing precision. LLMs, such as GPT-3 and GPT-4, have exhibited outstanding performance across a variety of tasks, from answering questions to writing essays and developing creative content.

LLMs employ deep learning techniques, notably neural networks, to evaluate language at various levels:

- **Contextual Understanding:** LLMs use sophisticated attention mechanisms to keep context across extended sections of text. This permits them to create logical and contextually relevant responses.

- **Fine-Tuning and Transfer Learning:** These models can be fine-tuned on certain jobs or industries, enabling them to specialize in fields such as healthcare, law, or finance.

- **Multilingual Capabilities:** Many LLMs are trained on data from many languages, allowing organizations to deploy them in diverse regions with minimal change.

The rise of LLMs has hastened the application of AI in business for various reasons:

- **Scalability:** Once trained, LLMs can be deployed at scale, managing a huge amount of inquiries, generating content, or assisting in customer service without the need for ongoing human interaction.

- **Cost Efficiency:** LLMs decrease the time and cost involved with manual content production, data analysis, and customer support by automating these activities.

- **Creativity Augmentation:** While LLMs do not replace human creativity, they can greatly improve it by generating recommendations, sketches, or even full frameworks that human workers can develop and adapt.

For organizations, this signifies a paradigm shift in how labor is conducted, as LLMs offer automation and creativity at levels previously impossible by typical AI systems.

1.3 Generative AI Market Growth and Future Projections

Generative AI is poised to become a cornerstone of technological innovation, with rapid growth projected across areas such as healthcare, entertainment, finance, and e-commerce. The technology's ability to improve efficiency, innovation, and cost savings has led to a spike in investments, with the global market for generative AI predicted to witness exponential development over the next decade.

Current Market Landscape:

According to industry reports, the global generative AI market size was valued at around **$8 billion in 2023** and is predicted to reach **$100+ billion by 2030.**

- Key drivers include increases in computer power, cloud infrastructure, and the rising availability of big datasets to train AI models.

- Industries such as **media and entertainment** have already embraced generative AI for content creation, while industries like **finance** are leveraging AI for fraud detection and automated reporting.

Key Sectors of Growth:

- **Healthcare:** AI-generated diagnoses, individualized treatment regimens, and drug development models are transforming the healthcare scene.

- **Retail and E-commerce:** Personalized suggestions, dynamic product displays, and automated customer service interactions enhance user experiences.

- **Manufacturing and Design:** Generative design is helping to build optimum goods by simulating numerous iterations based on design limitations and performance objectives.

- **Finance:** AI-driven reporting, insights, and fraud detection algorithms are making financial services faster, more accurate, and safe.

Future Trends in Generative AI:

- **Increased Personalization:** AI systems will grow more adept at adapting their outputs to individual users, generating hyper-personalized products, services, and information.

- **Human-AI Collaboration:** Rather of replacing humans, generative AI will increasingly operate in unison with human experts to increase productivity, creativity, and innovation.

- **Ethical and Regulatory Frameworks:** As generative AI grows more prevalent, the need for ethical frameworks and rules governing the technology will emerge. Issues such as data privacy, copyright, and misinformation will need to be addressed.

- **Real-Time AI Generation:** The future of generative AI will incorporate real-time content production, enabling organizations to respond immediately to changes in consumer behavior, market trends, or operational demands.

The introduction of generative AI signals a new chapter in commercial innovation. As the technology continues to evolve, its applications will proliferate, altering sectors and generating new opportunities for firms eager to accept it. Understanding its underlying concepts, the function of LLMs, and the broader market trends is crucial for firms trying to stay ahead in the competitive field. Generative AI offers the potential for greater creativity, automation, and business agility creating value across the whole organizational spectrum.

CHAPTER 2

LARGE LANGUAGE MODELS (LLMs) AND THEIR POWER

Large Language Models (LLMs) are among the most powerful developments in artificial intelligence. They have revolutionized natural language processing (NLP) and created new options for businesses to automate, personalize, and enhance their processes. In this chapter, we will look into how LLMs function, study their training methods and the relevance of accuracy in commercial use cases, and consider the future of LLMs with advancements like sparse expert models and self-improvement. Understanding these elements of LLMs will help organizations leverage their full potential and remain competitive in the changing AI world.

2.1 Understanding How LLMs Work

Large Language Models (LLMs) are developed on deep learning architectures, often utilizing neural networks with billions, or even trillions, of parameters. These models are designed to interpret, generate, and interact with human language. The underlying architecture is frequently built on the transformer model, a revolutionary paradigm unveiled in 2017, which allows LLMs to process enormous volumes of data and synthesize human-like language.

The Transformer Architecture:

1. At the center of LLMs is the transformer architecture, which leverages techniques such as self-attention to process input data. Unlike traditional models, transformers can analyze the complete context of a sentence or paragraph concurrently, rather than sequentially. This parallel processing power allows LLMs to manage huge volumes of input efficiently and provide coherent, contextually accurate results.

2. **Self-attention Mechanism:** This is an important aspect of transformers, allowing the model to "attend" to different portions of a sentence and balance their value when generating replies. This promotes sophisticated cognition, such as grasping complex concepts or resolving ambiguities in

language.

Language Generation:
- LLMs generate language by anticipating the next word in a sequence, based on the context provided by preceding words. Over time, students acquire the principles of grammar, syntax, and even more abstract components like tone, style, and inferred meaning. As a result, they are capable of generating text that can replicate human-written content across a number of domains and styles.

Fine-tuning and Specialization:
- While LLMs are trained on enormous quantities of generic data, they may also be fine-tuned to specialize in particular jobs or sectors. For example, a model can be fine-tuned for legal applications, healthcare diagnostics, or customer service by training it on domain-specific data. Fine-tuning boosts the accuracy and relevancy of the provided outputs for business-specific use cases.

The power of LLMs rests in their ability to interpret and

produce text at a scale and sophistication previously unthinkable. Their adaptability lets firms employ them across a variety of functions, from automating content generation to increasing customer care, giving a huge boost to productivity.

2.2 Training and Accuracy of LLMs in Business Use Cases

Training LLMs involves tremendous processing power, vast datasets, and advanced algorithms. The training process is crucial to the accuracy, reliability, and performance of LLMs, especially when implemented in corporate environments where precision is critical.

Training Process:
1. **Data Collection:** LLMs are often trained on vast datasets, spanning from publically available text (such as books, journals, and websites) to proprietary commercial data. The richness of this material is vital in shaping the LLM's ability to recognize context, meaning, and intricacies in language.
2. **Pre-training vs. Fine-tuning:** Pre-training entails

feeding the LLM with generic data to teach it the structure of human language, whereas fine-tuning optimizes the model for specific tasks by training it on targeted datasets. This two-stage procedure provides both broad language knowledge and task-specific accuracy.

3. **Gradient Descent and Backpropagation:** LLMs are optimized using a process called gradient descent, where the model adjusts its internal parameters (weights) based on errors encountered during training. Backpropagation is then used to fix these flaws by propagating them through the network, enabling the model to improve over time.

Accuracy and Evaluation:

1. The correctness of LLMs is tested by numerous evaluation metrics, including:
2. **Perplexity:** Measures how effectively the model anticipates the next word in a sequence. Lower confusion means more accuracy.
3. **BLEU (Bilingual Evaluation Understudy):** Commonly used for evaluating text production quality by comparing model outputs with reference

texts.

4. **F1 Score:** Particularly significant for classification tasks, this statistic combines precision and recall to determine the balance between false positives and false negatives.

For corporate use cases, accuracy is crucial. Whether it's automating customer service with chatbots or drafting legal documents, errors can have major ramifications. Businesses must carefully verify the correctness of LLMs in their unique area and ensure that models are fine-tuned for their individual needs. Human monitoring is often important to validate the results, especially in sensitive or high-stakes contexts.

Business Use Cases:
1. **Customer Service Automation:** LLMs can handle a large diversity of consumer queries, giving immediate, contextually relevant solutions. Fine-tuning the model for industry-specific vocabulary and circumstances enhances both accuracy and customer happiness.
2. **Content Creation:** From penning marketing emails

to preparing reports, LLMs can produce high-quality, human-like text at scale. However, assuring factual correctness and relevancy is vital, as LLMs may generate convincing but erroneous information.

3. **Data Analysis and Insights:** In fields like banking and healthcare, LLMs can aid with evaluating enormous amounts of textual data and deriving insights. Their accuracy in spotting trends, anomalies, or patterns directly impacts business decision-making.

The training procedure and accuracy of LLMs are crucial to their effectiveness in business applications. As businesses increasingly embrace these models, the ability to fine-tune them for specific activities will differentiate leaders from laggards in the AI-driven economy.

2.3 Future of LLMs: Sparse Expert Models and Self-Improvement

The future of Large Language Models is likely to be even more transformational, with upcoming ideas such as sparse expert models and self-improvement mechanisms set to revolutionize the AI environment.

Sparse Expert Models:
1. Traditional LLMs rely on dense designs where every layer of the model processes all incoming data. While this strategy has proven useful, it is computationally expensive and inefficient at scale. Sparse expert models offer a viable alternative by activating only a subset of the model's parameters (the "experts") based on the input.
2. **Dynamic Routing:** Sparse expert models employ dynamic routing algorithms that activate the most relevant elements of the model for a specific job. This eliminates computational cost and makes the model more efficient without sacrificing performance.
3. **Improved Scalability:** Sparse models can scale to bigger sizes more easily than dense models, as they do not require all parameters to be engaged at once. This is particularly helpful in corporate applications where real-time speed is crucial, such as in financial trading or automated customer contacts.

4. **Cost Efficiency:** Since less computational resources are utilized per operation, sparse expert models can considerably reduce the cost of adopting LLMs, making them more accessible to organizations of all sizes.

Self-Improvement Mechanisms:
1. Another fascinating advance in LLM technology is the concept of self-improving models. These models can continue learning from their interactions, evolving over time to increase their accuracy and relevance in real-world circumstances.
2. **Reinforcement Learning:** In self-improving models, reinforcement learning techniques are applied to allow the model to learn from feedback. For instance, an LLM used in customer service might gather input from consumers about the quality of responses, and over time, alter its outputs to better meet customer expectations.
3. **Continuous Fine-Tuning:** Unlike static models, self-improving LLMs can be fine-tuned continuously as they are exposed to new data. This is particularly beneficial in dynamic contexts where data changes

rapidly, such as stock markets or developing consumer preferences.

4. **Autonomous Improvement:** Self-improving models could potentially minimize the need for constant human interaction, as they autonomously update themselves depending on user feedback or fresh data inputs.

The merging of sparse expert models with self-improvement technologies marks the next step for LLMs, enabling organizations more efficient, adaptive, and powerful AI solutions. As LLMs get more efficient and autonomous, their applications will expand, allowing organizations the chance to harness AI in ways that were previously imagined.

Large Language Models are at the forefront of AI advancement, offering enterprises tremendous tools to automate and enhance processes across industries. By understanding how LLMs function, the importance of training and accuracy in commercial use cases, and the future improvements in sparse expert models and self-improvement, enterprises may position themselves to fully profit on this disruptive technology. As LLMs continue to evolve, their significance in business will further grow, unlocking new efficiencies, increasing user experiences, and driving innovation at an unprecedented rate.

CHAPTER 3

GENERATIVE AI IN MARKETING AND SALES

Generative AI is altering marketing and sales in significant ways, transforming how firms develop content, communicate with customers, and drive sales tactics. Leveraging AI-driven tools helps firms to optimize processes, personalize messaging, and forecast consumer behaviors with unsurpassed precision. This chapter discusses how generative AI is employed across marketing and sales, from providing high-quality content to increasing customer interactions and shaping predictive sales strategies.

3.1 AI-Generated Marketing Content: Text, Images, and Videos

Generative AI has changed content creation, offering marketers with the power to produce high-quality text, graphics, and videos at scale. These AI-driven solutions not only save time and costs but also enable for the rapid customisation and adaptation of content to match individual audience needs. Let's analyze how generative AI impacts these three primary categories of marketing content.

Text Generation:
1. AI technologies such as OpenAI's GPT models, Jasper, and Writesonic can generate attractive written material, including blog posts, product descriptions, email campaigns, social media updates, and more. These models are trained on large quantities of data and can write in numerous tones, voices, and formats, making them useful across diverse industries.
2. **Personalization at Scale:** Marketers can employ AI to tailor content for certain customer categories. By evaluating user data, AI may generate personalized emails or social media posts that resonate with individual interests, resulting in increased engagement and conversion rates.
3. **SEO Optimization:** AI-generated content can be developed to enhance search engine rankings by

including relevant keywords, enhancing readability, and ensuring that articles are aligned with current SEO standards. This leads to improved web presence and higher organic visitors.

Image Generation:
1. Tools like DALL-E and MidJourney allow marketers to produce bespoke images based on specific text prompts. This is especially beneficial for businesses trying to develop visually compelling content without relying on stock photographs or expensive photo shoots.
2. **Branding Consistency:** AI-generated graphics may be adjusted to meet a brand's color scheme, style, and tone, ensuring that marketing visuals remain constant across numerous platforms and campaigns.
3. **Dynamic Visual Content:** With generative AI, firms may develop several variations of product pictures for different demographics or areas. For instance, a clothing firm may develop several photos of the same product but stylized to appeal to various cultural aesthetics.

Video Creation:
1. AI-powered platforms like Synthesia and Pictory are capable of generating videos from text prompts or minimum input, substantially decreasing the resources and time necessary for video production. These tools can make explainer videos, ads, or lessons that feel professional and engaging.
2. **AI-Driven Personalization:** In video marketing, generative AI can assist develop personalized video messages for certain client segments or even individual customers. By evaluating customer data, AI can automatically customize video content to fit the viewer's interests, boosting the relevancy and effectiveness of the message.
3. **Scaling Video Campaigns**: Marketers can now scale their video campaigns by automating the generation of several versions for various platforms (e.g., YouTube, Instagram, TikTok). This enables marketers to swiftly modify their messaging and visual style for each platform's distinct audience and format.

Incorporating generative AI into marketing content

development offers for unprecedented speed, efficiency, and originality. It boosts the capacity to target specific audience segments with individualized information, creating a more immersive and engaging consumer experience.

3.2 Customer Engagement: Conversational AI and Chatbots

Customer engagement is a vital component of marketing and sales success. With the rise of conversational AI and chatbots, businesses can now engage customers in real-time, give quick help, and deliver personalized suggestions at any step of the customer experience. Conversational AI boosts both the customer experience and operational efficiency, since it minimizes the need for human intervention while maintaining high levels of satisfaction.

Conversational AI and Natural Language Processing (NLP):

1. Conversational AI platforms, such as IBM Watson Assistant and Google Dialogflow, are powered by

NLP technologies that allow machines to understand and interpret human language. These AI systems are capable of holding meaningful interactions with clients, answering questions, resolving issues, and leading users through complex tasks.

2. **24/7 Availability:** One of the key advantages of conversational AI is its capacity to give help around the clock, ensuring that clients have access to information or assistance whenever they need it. This can drastically minimize customer churn and enhance satisfaction levels.

3. **Enhanced Personalization:** By assessing past interactions, purchasing history, and user preferences, conversational AI may give highly tailored responses and recommendations. For example, an AI-driven chatbot may propose products based on a customer's browsing activity, thus enhancing the likelihood of a sale.

Chatbots in Sales and Support:

1. **Lead Generation and Qualification:** AI chatbots play a vital role in sales, notably in lead creation and qualification. When integrated into a company's

website, chatbots may engage visitors, ask pertinent questions to discover their needs, and qualify leads by gathering vital information. Qualified leads are then sent on to human sales teams, expediting the sales pipeline.

2. **Product Recommendations and Upselling:** Chatbots can also be used to assist the sales process by delivering personalized product recommendations based on the customer's past purchases or current inquiry. This type of automated upselling boosts the average order value and gives a more personalized shopping experience.

3. **Customer Support Automation:** AI-powered chatbots are capable of addressing a wide range of customer support requests, from resolving technical difficulties to answering FAQs. For more difficult situations, the chatbot can smoothly shift the conversation to a human agent, ensuring that the customer's demands are handled efficiently.

Voice Assistants in Marketing:

1. Voice assistants like Amazon Alexa, Google Assistant, and Siri are becoming crucial tools for

brands trying to engage customers through voice interactions. Marketers can develop speech-enabled experiences, such as voice-search optimized content, voice-controlled applications, or interactive voice ads, which provide a more immersive and engaging consumer journey.

2. **Voice Commerce (V-Commerce):** As voice assistants grow increasingly popular, the concept of voice commerce is gaining steam. Consumers may now use voice commands to search for products, place purchases, and manage subscriptions, offering a frictionless buying experience. Brands are increasingly embracing AI-driven voice tactics to capture this rising sector of the market.

In short, conversational AI and chatbots are revolutionizing how organizations engage with their customers, making interactions more efficient, tailored, and accessible. These solutions help firms to keep ongoing engagement with their customers, enhancing satisfaction and encouraging conversions.

3.3 Predictive Sales Strategies Using AI

Predictive sales methods, enabled by AI, are transforming the way firms approach their sales operations. AI-powered algorithms can analyze massive volumes of data to find trends, forecast customer behavior, and enhance sales efforts. By employing predictive analytics, firms may increase decision-making, streamline sales operations, and anticipate client wants with unparalleled accuracy.

AI-Driven Sales Forecasting:
1. Predictive analytics can examine previous sales data, consumer demographics, purchasing behaviors, and market trends to estimate future sales performance. AI algorithms find patterns and connections that may be difficult for human analysts to detect, offering sales teams with more accurate and actionable projections.
2. **Demand Forecasting:** AI helps organizations forecast demand swings by evaluating seasonality, market patterns, and external variables such as economic situations. With these insights, organizations may better manage inventory, optimize

production, and reduce expenses associated with overproduction or stockouts.

3. **Sales Pipeline Optimization:** AI-driven systems can assess every stage of the sales pipeline, revealing potential bottlenecks and areas of improvement. For instance, AI might indicate where prospects are dropping off or where conversion rates are low, allowing sales teams to make data-driven improvements to their strategy.

Predictive Lead Scoring and Prioritization:

1. Predictive lead scoring uses AI to evaluate and rank leads based on their propensity to convert into paying clients. By assessing criteria such as lead behavior, engagement levels, and demographic data, AI can assign ratings to each lead, enabling sales people prioritize their efforts on the most promising prospects.

2. **Improved Sales Efficiency:** With predictive lead scoring, sales teams may focus on high-value leads, reducing the time spent on cold or unqualified prospects. This raises overall efficiency and improves the possibilities of closing business.

3. **Behavioral Analytics:** AI can track customer behavior across different touchpoints—website visits, email clicks, social media interactions—and use this data to estimate the chance of conversion. This allows sales teams to engage with leads at the ideal time, boosting the odds of success.

Personalized Sales Campaigns:
1. AI allows sales teams to design highly personalized campaigns suited to specific customer demands and preferences. By evaluating consumer data, AI can advise the optimum time to reach out, the style of messaging that resonates with the customer, and the most relevant items or services to offer.
2. **Predictive Content Suggestions:** AI systems can examine what sorts of content have been most effective in engaging a particular customer and suggest future content to generate more interaction. For instance, if a consumer responds positively to product demo videos, AI can propose sending them a new product instructional to enhance interest and drive toward conversion.
3. **Dynamic price:** AI may optimize price strategies by

assessing market conditions, competitive pricing, and client demand. Predictive models can recommend optimal pricing points to optimize profits while remaining competitive, and they can also trigger price adjustments in real-time to capitalize on market developments.

AI-driven predictive sales methods give businesses with better insights into their sales operations, allowing them to make wiser decisions, increase client connections, and improve overall sales success. Predictive analytics helps sales teams to anticipate consumer behavior, optimize their outreach efforts, and create highly personalized experiences that promote long-term success.

Generative AI is rapidly altering the disciplines of marketing and sales, offering organizations with new tools to develop compelling content, communicate with customers more efficiently, and predict sales patterns with more precision. By integrating AI-generated content, conversational AI, and predictive sales methods, firms can stay ahead of the competition, boost customer satisfaction, and drive revenue growth. This new era of AI-driven marketing and sales not only enhances productivity but also provides more meaningful, tailored customer experiences.

CHAPTER 4

USING GENERATIVE AI IN PRODUCT DEVELOPMENT AND OPERATIONS

Generative AI is proving to be an effective tool for expediting the development of new products and optimizing operations. AI is changing how companies run their internal processes and launch goods by automating customer service, spotting production irregularities, and streamlining documentation. With an emphasis on automating processes that historically needed a large amount of manual input, this chapter examines the uses of AI in operational efficiency and product innovation.

4.1 AI Chatbots for Automating Customer Support

Customer service is essential in today's corporate climate to preserve solid client relationships and guarantee high satisfaction levels. With their round-the-clock availability, quick response times, and customized interactions,

AI-powered chatbots have become a game-changer for automating customer support. These chatbots are made to answer a variety of issues, from simple inquiries to more intricate troubleshooting, which helps companies save money on operations while improving customer satisfaction.

1. **The following is real-time assistance:** The capacity of AI chatbots to offer clients real-time support is among their greatest benefits. Chatbots are always accessible to answer simple questions, handle returns, or walk customers through troubleshooting procedures, cutting down on wait times and increasing customer satisfaction.
2. **Availability: 24/7:** Businesses may provide round-the-clock support using AI-powered solutions, guaranteeing that clients get help whenever they need it, regardless of time zones or office hours. This is especially beneficial for multinational corporations that cater to a variety of markets.

Improving Efficiency and Reducing Costs:

1. Chatbots allow human agents to concentrate on more

difficult or high-value issues by automating repetitive jobs like answering frequently asked questions (FAQs). This increases the customer service team's overall productivity and lessens the requirement for heavy personnel during busy times.

2. **Cost Reduction:** By reducing the need for huge customer care personnel, AI chatbots help cut operating costs. With the ability to manage hundreds or even thousands of interactions at once, a single chatbot can significantly cut labor expenses and eliminate the need to hire more employees.

Personalized Customer conversations:

1. AI chatbots can analyze user behavior, past purchases, and preferences to personalize conversations. This enables companies to provide clients with more individualized help, make recommendations that are specific to them, and fix problems more quickly.

2. Natural language processing (NLP) at its most advanced: NLP capabilities in contemporary AI chatbots allow them to accurately comprehend and interpret consumer inquiries. This enables them to

have deep discussions, provide pertinent answers, and help clients navigate increasingly challenging situations.

Effortless Transition to Human Agents:
1. AI chatbots are excellent at answering standard questions, but they can also recognize when a problem calls for human assistance. By offering context and guaranteeing a seamless transition, the chatbot may smoothly move the discussion to a human agent when confronted with a more delicate or sophisticated query.
2. **Models of Hybrid Support**: Nowadays, a lot of companies employ hybrid models in which chatbots manage first encounters and human agents only step in when required. This guarantees that clients receive individualized, superior care while lessening the workload for human agents.

AI chatbots are transforming customer service by cutting costs and providing quicker, more individualized assistance. They guarantee that companies can offer effective, superior customer service on a large scale, which is essential for preserving competitive advantage in the current market.

4.2 Using AI to Find Production Errors and Anomalies

Ensuring product quality and consistency is of utmost importance in manufacturing and production settings. In order to assist organizations avoid expensive mistakes, cut waste, and maintain excellent product quality, AI-driven solutions are being utilized more and more to identify abnormalities and faults during the production process. Businesses may boost overall product reliability, decrease downtime, and increase operational efficiency by utilizing AI for anomaly detection.

Visual Inspection Driven by AI:
1. Manual inspection has historically been a major component of quality control, but it may be laborious, prone to human mistake, and challenging to scale. On the other hand, AI-based visual inspection systems automatically identify flaws in goods or components as they pass through the manufacturing line using computer vision and

machine learning algorithms.

2. **Defect Detection in Real Time:** Real-time product picture or video analysis by these systems can identify any irregularities that might point to flaws. This lowers the possibility that customers will receive faulty products by allowing manufacturers to take prompt corrective action.

3. **More Precision:** Even the smallest flaws that the human eye could overlook can be found by AI systems. These systems can gradually increase their detection accuracy by learning from production data, guaranteeing constant quality control.

Predictive Maintenance:

1. By evaluating data from machinery and equipment to detect possible issues before they happen, artificial intelligence (AI) also plays a crucial part in predictive maintenance. Artificial intelligence (AI) algorithms can forecast when a machine is likely to break and send out maintenance alerts by tracking key performance indicators (KPIs) including temperature, vibration, and operating efficiency.

2. **Minimizing Downtime:** By minimizing unplanned

equipment failures, predictive maintenance lowers downtime and guarantees uninterrupted output. This proactive strategy increases overall operational efficiency and results in significant cost savings.

3. AI is also capable of optimizing maintenance schedules, which guarantees the efficient allocation of resources. By scheduling maintenance tasks during times when production demand is low, disturbance can be minimized and productivity can be increased.

Using AI Algorithms to Automate Quality Control:

1. In addition to eye inspection, AI can be used to detect production abnormalities by analyzing data from sensors, Internet of Things devices, and other sources. Manufacturers can identify trends that could point to problems with the production process, including variations in temperature, pressure, or material composition, thanks to this data-driven approach.

2. **Ongoing Enhancement:** Early anomaly detection allows manufacturers to make constant process improvements, modifying settings and streamlining

operations to guarantee peak performance. This results in more effective production, less waste, and better-quality products.

AI integration into industrial processes increases overall operational efficiency in addition to improving fault detection speed and accuracy. Businesses may cut expenses, enhance product quality, and keep a competitive advantage in the market by implementing AI-powered anomaly detection and predictive maintenance.

4.3 Automating User Manuals and Product Documentation

User manuals and product documentation are essential parts of any product lifecycle because they give consumers the knowledge they need to maintain, operate, and troubleshoot their devices. However, it might take a lot of work and effort to create and manage these papers. A large portion of this process may be automated by generative AI, which would make it simpler for companies to produce accurate, current documentation that enhances user experience.

Documentation Generated by AI:

1. AI can automatically create product documentation, such as installation instructions, technical manuals, and user guides, using natural language generation (NLG) technology. These systems create clear, succinct, and educational papers that assist users with a variety of activities by analyzing user data, product specs, and other pertinent information.

2. **Adapting Documentation to Various Audiences:** AI is able to customize documents for various user groups. For instance, it can produce more thorough technical instructions for professionals or advanced users and simplified user guides for novices. This guarantees that every user gets the right amount of advice depending on their requirements.

3. **The process of automating updates:** Maintaining product documentation current with updates or new versions is one of the biggest issues. AI can ensure that users always have access to the most recent information by automatically updating documentation as products change.

Improving User Experience with Dynamic User Guides:

1. AI-generated documentation can be included into digital platforms, such websites or mobile apps, to provide users with real-time, interactive support. This enhances the user experience. For example, consumers could engage with an AI-powered guide that guides them through particular tasks depending on their present needs rather than going through a long handbook.

2. **Contextual support:** By examining user behavior and making recommendations or offering direction based on the tasks a user is performing, AI-powered systems are able to offer contextual support. For instance, the system might automatically show pertinent instructions or troubleshooting advice if a user is having problems with a specific feature.

3. **Integration of Multimedia:** Multimedia documentation, such as interactive manuals, animated lessons, and instructional movies, can also be created using generative AI. These dynamic resources improve users' overall experience by providing a more thorough and interesting manner for them to learn about a product.

Simplifying Translation and Localization:
1. To address a varied consumer base, multinational corporations must provide product documentation in several languages. AI-powered translation technologies can automate the localization process, accurately and culturally relevantly translating user manuals and instructions into many languages.
2. **Consistency in All Markets:** Businesses may lower the possibility of mistakes or misunderstandings by employing AI to oversee the localization process and guarantee that their product documentation is similar across regions.

Decreased Workload for Product Teams:
1. AI greatly lessens the effort for product development and support teams by automating the creation and upkeep of product documentation. Teams are able to concentrate on higher-value activities as a result, like refining the product or answering more intricate client questions.
2. **Improved Scalability:** AI can automatically create the necessary documentation when firms expand and

introduce new goods or upgrades, allowing them to stay up with expanding product lines without overburdening their workforce.

Companies can increase the quality of their documentation, expedite the process, and improve the user experience by implementing AI-driven automation of product documentation and user manuals. Businesses may guarantee that their product information is always correct, current, and available to a worldwide audience by utilizing generative AI.

By automating crucial procedures like customer service, production anomaly detection, and product documentation, generative AI is revolutionizing operations and product creation. Businesses may increase productivity, cut expenses, and enhance product quality with these AI-powered solutions. AI's influence on operations and product development will only increase as it develops further, allowing businesses to innovate more quickly and provide greater value to their clients.

CHAPTER 5

ENGINEERING AND IT APPLICATIONS OF GENERATIVE AI

By automating processes, increasing development speed, and boosting accuracy in data management and coding, generative AI is transforming the domains of engineering and information technology. AI tools are increasingly widely used in data management, software development, and creative problem-solving, going beyond mere task automation. This chapter will explore how AI-assisted coding tools, such as GitHub Copilot, are revolutionizing software development, how AI can manage data tables and massive datasets, and how AI improves productivity by automating code generation.

5.1 Software Development and Coding Aided by AI

A significant advancement in software development is represented by AI-assisted coding, in which programmers use AI to write code that is cleaner, more dependable, and more efficient. AI is allowing developers to work more quickly and accurately by eliminating tedious chores, making suggestions for improvements, and even spotting possible faults or vulnerabilities.

1. **Improving the Productivity of Developers:** The increased efficiency of developers is one of the biggest effects of AI-assisted coding. AI solutions allow developers to concentrate more on solving complicated problems than on manual coding tasks by offering real-time suggestions, code autocompletion, and best practice recommendations.

2. **Autocompletion and Code Suggestions:** These days, AI coding assistants are able to understand the context of the code, anticipate the developer's next move, and provide insightful code recommendations. In addition to accelerating the coding process, this also lessens typos and grammatical problems.

3. **Boilerplate Code Reduction:** Boilerplate code is repetitive but required code that developers frequently spend a lot of time writing. This code can be automatically generated by AI technologies, freeing up developers to focus on more important project components.

4. **Debugging in Real Time:** Syntax mistakes, runtime errors, and possible security flaws can be identified in real-time by AI-powered tools before the developer even executes the code. This guarantees that programming is more dependable from the start by drastically cutting down on debugging time.

Speeding Up Learning for Novice Developers:
1. AI-assisted coding is another effective tool for novice or less experienced developers. These tools serve as mentors and assistants, assisting developers in learning new languages, frameworks, and coding methodologies more quickly by providing recommendations and explanations for intricate algorithms.
2. **Interactive Education:** The interactive learning experience offered by AI tools, which provide instant feedback, provide improvement suggestions, and explain why some code snippets are better, is beneficial for novice coders. This helps developers establish solid basic coding abilities and speeds up the learning curve.
3. **Code Documentation and Examples:** In addition to

providing fast access to the information required to finish a task, AI tools can produce pertinent code examples in response to a developer's question and link to official documentation.

Improving Code Quality:
1. AI-assisted tools enhance code quality in addition to speed. AI assists developers in writing cleaner, more effective code by recommending best practices for architecture, security, and coding.
2. **Code Refactoring:** Code that can be rewritten or optimized for improved performance can be automatically detected using AI tools. For example, they can offer simpler methods to arrange code blocks, lessen unnecessary code, or suggest more effective algorithms.
3. **Security Improvements:** AI can assist developers in making sure their code is secure from the beginning by identifying vulnerabilities and suggesting patches, including typical security problems like SQL injection and cross-site scripting.

5.2 GitHub Copilot: Automating Code to Cut Down on Development Time

GitHub Developers' approach to coding chores is being revolutionized by Copilot, an AI-powered tool created by OpenAI in collaboration with GitHub. Copilot is now a valuable tool for developers trying to increase productivity and cut down on development time because it can generate code snippets, suggest functions, and automate repetitive activities.

GitHub Copilot's Operation:
1. GitHub Based on developer comments and code inputs, Copilot generates code using a machine learning model more precisely, a variant of OpenAI's GPT-3. It can anticipate the developer's goals and recommend whole functions or approaches that align with them.
2. **Contextual Knowledge:** Copilot's comprehension of the code's context is among its most remarkable features. For instance, Copilot will recommend JavaScript functions and methods that are pertinent to the task at hand if a developer is working on a

JavaScript project. It works very well for both small and large jobs because of its contextual awareness.

Speeding Up Code Writing:

1. GitHub Writing code takes a lot less time while using Copilot. Developers only need to use plain English to explain a function, and Copilot will produce the appropriate code. This lessens the need to look for related code snippets in manuals or on StackOverflow.

2. **Functions Completed from Comments:** Complete functions can be automatically generated by Copilot using developer comments. For example, Copilot will produce the relevant code for a function if a developer puts a comment like // **Function to calculate factorial.**

3. **Multilingual Compatibility:** Among the various programming languages that Copilot supports are Python, JavaScript, TypeScript, Ruby, Go, and many more. Because of its adaptability, developers working on multilingual projects or in various locations might benefit greatly from it.

Reducing Repetitive Coding Tasks:
1. The ability of Copilot to automate repetitive coding activities, like loop creation, error message processing, and CRUD (Create, Read, Update, Delete) processes in database applications, is a great advantage. Developers save time and lower the possibility of making mistakes by having this kind of boilerplate code generated automatically.
2. **Using IDEs for Integration:** Developers may easily integrate Copilot into their workflow because it interacts directly with well-known integrated programming environments (IDEs), such as Visual Studio Code. By incorporating AI recommendations straight into the development environment, this integration speeds up coding even further.

Ethical considerations and possible limitations:
1. Despite its many advantages, Copilot has drawbacks. Developers must check the AI-generated code to make sure it complies with the project's specifications because it may occasionally produce inaccurate or subpar code.
2. **The Use of AI-Generated Code in an Ethical**

Way: The usage of AI-generated code raises additional ethical issues, namely with regard to ownership and licensing. Developers are responsible for making sure the created code does not breach license agreements or copyrights.

5.3 Using AI to Create and Complete Data Tables

An essential part of engineering and IT projects is data management and analysis. In order to handle big information, find trends, and derive useful insights, artificial intelligence (AI) has emerged as a crucial tool for automating the production and completion of data tables. AI solutions can fill in missing values, forecast future data trends, and even generate complete datasets from preexisting information by analyzing data using machine learning models.

The following is an example of AI-assisted data entry and completion:
Data entry is frequently laborious and prone to mistakes. By employing algorithms to find patterns in the data that is already available and forecast missing values or entire

rows of data based on the trends it finds, artificial intelligence (AI) can automate this process.

1. **Managing Absent Information:** By examining the connections between various data points, AI may complete missing values in a dataset. For instance, AI can forecast the missing numbers based on other variables like the order date, shipping method, and distance to the destination if a dataset of client orders has missing delivery timeframes.

2. **Decrease in Human Error:** AI greatly lowers the possibility of human error by automating data entry, guaranteeing the accuracy and completeness of the datasets. For huge datasets, where human entry would be laborious and prone to errors, this is very helpful.

Predictive Data Analysis:

1. AI is capable of more than just filling out data tables; it can also examine the data and forecast future patterns. AI, for example, can forecast future sales volumes by evaluating past sales data, which helps firms anticipate demand and make wise decisions.

2. Businesses are able to make smarter, data-driven decisions thanks to AI-driven data completeness. AI, for instance, can assist a business in identifying which products, based on current market patterns, are likely to be in high demand, resulting in more effective production planning and inventory management.

Creating Data Tables Automatically:

1. AI can help create completely new datasets in addition to filling in already-existing tables. AI can create new tables that highlight important trends or offer useful insights by examining connected data points. AI might, for instance, produce a table that records past purchases made by customers and highlights trends in their purchasing habits.

2. **Converting Unstructured Data into Formats That Can Be Used**: Additionally, unstructured data such text or image data can be analyzed by AI systems and converted into organized formats, like databases or tables. Businesses wishing to examine data from a variety of sources, such as social media, customer evaluations, or sensor data, may find this capacity to

be extremely useful.

To improve data accuracy and consistency, artificial intelligence (AI) methods can also be employed to make sure that data tables are error-free and consistent. AI can detect inconsistencies and standardize data formats by cross-referencing data from various sources, enhancing the dataset's overall quality.

- **Validation of Data and Error Checking:** In order to identify any problems before they affect analytical or decision-making processes, AI-driven data validation systems can automatically check for outliers, wrong entries, or inconsistencies.

By automating crucial coding, software development, and data management processes, generative AI is revolutionizing the engineering and IT industries. While AI-driven data tools are improving the correctness and consistency of data tables, AI-assisted coding tools, such as GitHub Copilot, are cutting down on development time by creating and optimizing code. Engineers and developers can now concentrate on solving complicated problems instead of wasting time on tedious or error-prone jobs thanks to these advancements, which are also increasing productivity and quality of work. AI's significance in engineering and IT will only grow as the technology develops, spurring more creativity and efficiency in these vital sectors.

CHAPTER 6

LEGAL AND RISK CONSIDERATIONS FOR GENERATIVE AI

The introduction of generative AI is causing major changes in the legal and risk management industries. By automating repetitive chores, enhancing compliance, and offering insights into massive volumes of legal data, these cutting-edge solutions improve accuracy, streamline procedures, and reduce risks. This chapter examines the ways in which generative AI is being used to efficiently manage contracts and patents, summarize legal developments, and draft and review legal documents.

6.1 Automatically Drafting and Examining Legal Documents

Legal document drafting has always been a time-consuming procedure demanding a high level of skill and meticulousness. By automating the production and evaluation of legal papers, generative AI is now transforming the field. This not only increases productivity but also lowers the possibility of mistakes.

Automated Document Drafting: AI-powered technologies can create legal documents, including agreements, contracts, and briefs, using input data and pre-established templates. In order to generate papers that satisfy particular legal criteria, these technologies make use of machine learning and natural language processing (NLP) to comprehend the subtleties of legal terminology.

- **Customization of the Template:** Templates can be altered by generative AI to meet user requirements. For instance, a lawyer can enter information about the parties, duration, and particular provisions if they are required to construct a non-disclosure agreement (NDA). The AI then saves time and effort by creating a customized document that includes these components.
- **Language Consistency:** Law companies may guarantee uniformity in language and vocabulary across all legal papers by using AI to draft documents. This is especially crucial for preserving the accuracy of legal terminology and minimizing

misinterpretations in contracts.

Automated Document Review: AI systems can help with legal document review by spotting errors, inconsistencies, and compliance problems. These technologies, for example, can point up linguistic errors, improper clause positions, or omitted details that might give rise to legal issues.

- **Accuracy and Speed:** AI greatly expedites the review of documents. AI can analyze vast amounts of text in a matter of seconds, giving lawyers insightful advice on what needs to be changed or what needs more focus. Because of this efficiency, attorneys can avoid becoming bogged down in document review and instead concentrate on more strategic work.

The mitigation of risks: AI lowers the possibility of human error, which can result in expensive legal battles, by automating the drafting and review process. Potential hazards linked to unclear wording or provisions that might not adhere to existing rules and regulations might be identified by the tools.

- **Exercise Due Diligence:** For instance, AI can assist with due diligence in mergers and acquisitions by automatically examining a large number of legal papers to find potential risks or liabilities. This enables businesses to base their decisions on thorough data analysis and make better informed choices.

6.2 Highlighting and Recapitulating Legal Developments

It can be difficult for legal practitioners to stay on top of constantly changing laws and regulations. Legal staff can stay educated and compliant by using generative AI to automate the summarization of pertinent information and make it easier to monitor changes in the law.

Legal practitioners can more easily and rapidly understand important information by using AI systems that can evaluate long legal documents, case laws, and regulation texts to extract and summarize crucial aspects.

- **The process of natural language processing:** AI can recognize significant changes in laws or regulations and provide succinct descriptions of them using NLP techniques. For legal teams who need to keep abreast of developments that can affect their practice areas, this capability is vital.

Highlighting Important Legal Changes: AI is able to monitor and draw attention to pertinent modifications to laws and rules, enabling legal practitioners to recognize and quickly adjust to these changes. This competence is essential in areas like corporate law and compliance, where breaking new rules can lead to serious consequences.

- **Customized News:** Legal practitioners can receive customized updates from generative AI according to their practice areas. For instance, an employment lawyer would be notified of modifications to labor laws, while a corporate lawyer might receive alerts and summaries concerning changes in business law.

Impact on Compliance:

- AI improves compliance initiatives in enterprises by emphasizing and summarizing legislative changes. Legal teams can lower the risk of non-compliance by making sure that their procedures and policies reflect the most recent legal requirements.

- **Education and Training:** By giving legal professionals instant access to the most recent legal developments and their ramifications, AI can also help with training and education. This guarantees that every team member is aware of the latest information and is able to use it efficiently in their work.

6.3 Using AI to Manage Patents and Contracts

One crucial area where generative AI can be extremely beneficial is in the administration of patents and contracts. Artificial intelligence (AI) solutions can optimize the whole patent and contract lifecycle, from invention to monitoring and enforcement, increasing productivity and lowering risks.

The entire contract management process, from drafting to execution and compliance monitoring, can be automated with the aid of artificial intelligence (AI) solutions. By using user inputs and pre-existing templates, these tools may create contracts that contain all required clauses.

1. **The analysis of contracts:** AI is capable of examining current contracts to find important terms, responsibilities, and any hazards. In large firms with many contracts to manage, where human analysis would be laborious and prone to errors, this capacity is quite helpful.
2. **Tracking Performance:** Organizations can use AI to track contract performance and terms and conditions compliance. Organizations can stay in compliance with their contractual responsibilities by using AI tools to set notifications for important deadlines, milestones, and renewal dates.

Patent administration:
1. By automating the patent application process, doing prior art searches, and examining patent portfolios, generative AI can help with patent administration in the field of intellectual property.
2. **Search for Patents Automatically**: AI can find existing patents that might affect a new application by doing thorough searches across patent databases. This feature facilitates the patent application process and helps businesses steer clear of possible

infringement problems.

3. **Portfolio Evaluation:** By evaluating a patent's advantages and disadvantages, spotting possible licensing opportunities, and proposing tactics for patent enforcement, AI can also help manage patent portfolios.

Compliance and Risk Assessment:

1. By assessing contracts and patents for possible legal liability, AI improves risk assessment. AI technologies enable legal teams to proactively handle problems before they worsen by spotting unclear terminology or clauses that could spark disagreements.

2. **Encouraging Cooperation:** AI solutions can also make it easier for business, legal, and compliance teams to work together. AI makes sure that everyone involved is on the same page and aware of their rights and responsibilities under the law by making contract and patent information easily accessible.

By automating the creation and evaluation of legal papers, summarizing legislative developments, and expediting contract and patent management procedures, generative AI is revolutionizing the legal and risk management industries. By improving efficiency, accuracy, and compliance, these innovations free up legal professionals to concentrate on higher-value work that calls for knowledge and strategic thinking. As generative AI technology develops further, its application in the legal industry has the potential to revolutionize the provision of legal services by enabling businesses to more confidently and nimbly negotiate the complexity of risk and the law.

CHAPTER 7

HUMAN RESOURCES (HR) AND GENERATIVE AI

The way businesses handle their workforces could be completely transformed by the incorporation of generative AI into HR. AI-driven solutions may optimize HR operations, improve decision-making, and foster a more engaged workforce by streamlining hiring procedures, automating administrative duties, and boosting employee experiences. This chapter explores how generative AI is enhancing onboarding and staff management, automating HR procedures, and changing applicant assessments.

7.1 AI-Driven Interview Questions for Evaluating Candidates

The hiring process is frequently laborious and full of difficulties, such as the possibility of subjectivity and bias in candidate assessments. By creating customized interview questions that evaluate abilities, experience, and cultural fit, generative AI can improve candidate evaluations.

Developing Tailored Interview Questions:

1. In order to create personalized interview questions, generative AI can examine job descriptions, resumes, and corporate culture. HR managers can guarantee a more focused evaluation of applicants by coordinating inquiries with the particular demands of a position.

2. **Questions Particular to Skills:** For example, the AI can produce questions that assess particular abilities, such as coding competence for software development roles or analytical thinking for data analysis roles, if a job calls for technical knowledge. Better recruiting decisions result from this focused strategy, which guarantees that interviews evaluate pertinent competencies.

Standardizing Evaluations:

1. Standardizing interview questions for all candidates is one benefit of utilizing AI in candidate assessments. Because each applicant is assessed

using the same standards, this consistency reduces the possibility of prejudice and encourages equity in the recruiting process.

2. **Minimizing Prejudice:** By emphasizing candidates' credentials and abilities above their personal traits, AI can likewise lessen unconscious bias. A more inclusive and varied workforce may result from this unbiased approach.

Assessing the Responses of Candidates: In addition to creating questions, AI can instantly evaluate applicants' answers to reveal information about their critical thinking, communication, and compatibility with company values. The language used, the tone, and the general coherence of the responses are some of the variables that may serve as the basis for this study.

- **Recommendations and feedback:** Based on candidates' answers, the AI can also give interviewers comments and suggestions that highlight their advantages and disadvantages. When deciding which applicants to move on in the employment process, HR professionals can use this input to make better decisions.

7.2 Self-Serve Solutions for HR Process Automation

By automating repetitive procedures, generative AI may optimize HR operations and free up HR experts to concentrate on more strategic projects. AI-powered self-serve systems can improve worker satisfaction and boost productivity.

Self-Service Portals:

1. AI-driven self-service portals let staff members get information and finish tasks on their own. This covers handling personal data, obtaining benefits, requesting time off, and locating solutions to commonly asked concerns.
2. **24/7 Availability:** Regardless of time zones or office hours, employees may get immediate answers to their questions when AI chatbots are integrated into these portals. This accessibility lessens the effort for HR departments while also improving employee happiness.

Automating Administrative processes: AI-driven

systems can automate routine administrative processes including benefits enrollment, payroll processing, and compliance monitoring. In addition to improving productivity, this automation lowers the possibility of errors that come with human processes.

- **Simplified Processes:** For example, by integrating with business processes to guarantee regulatory compliance, AI may automate the approval process for time-off requests. HR teams can focus on more important projects as a result of the time and resource savings from this workflow simplification.

Insights Driven by Data:

- AI systems are able to evaluate employee data and offer useful insights on employee engagement, turnover rates, and workforce trends. HR managers may improve employee happiness and retention by using these insights to inform their actions.
- The use of predictive analytics AI is able to recognize patterns and trends using predictive analytics that could point to possible problems, such excessive employee turnover or discontent. By taking early measures to resolve these problems

before they worsen, HR departments can encourage a more engaged staff.

7.3 Enhancing Employee Management and Onboarding

For new hires to succeed and stay engaged over the long term, the onboarding process is essential. Generative AI can help with continuous personnel management and improve onboarding experiences.

Personalized Onboarding Experiences:
1. Generative AI is able to develop customized onboarding programs based on the role, abilities, and prior experiences of every new hire. Organizations may make sure that new hires feel prepared and supported right away by offering pertinent tools and training materials.
2. In order to engage new personnel during the onboarding process, AI-driven platforms can provide interactive learning modules. This could include training movies, virtual tours, and tests that improve knowledge and recall of business policies and processes.

By collecting feedback from workers at different phases of their onboarding and employment cycle, artificial intelligence (AI) solutions may support continuous employee engagement. Performance reviews, pulse checks, and surveys can all be used to get this input.

- **Real-Time Modifications:** AI solutions can assist HR managers in identifying areas for onboarding process improvement and making real-time adjustments by analyzing comments. Retention is encouraged and the entire work experience is improved by this responsiveness.

Performance Management:

1. By automating goal-setting, progress monitoring, and employee feedback, generative AI can help with performance management. AI-powered performance management solutions can assist managers and HR specialists in establishing reasonable objectives based on past performance and industry standards.

2. **Data-Driven Assessments:** AI can examine performance data to find patterns and trends, enabling more accurate assessments and helpful criticism. Organizations may make well-informed

decisions on career development opportunities, training requirements, and promotions thanks to this data-driven strategy.

By boosting onboarding and staff management, automating HR procedures, and improving applicant assessments, generative AI is revolutionizing the human resources industry. Organizations may improve employee experiences, expedite processes, and make data-driven decisions that promote a more engaged and effective workforce by utilizing AI-driven solutions. AI's incorporation with HR procedures is probably going to get more complex as it develops, significantly streamlining HR operations and promoting organizational performance.

CHAPTER 8

USING GENERATIVE AI TO OPTIMIZE EMPLOYEES AND UTILITY

In a variety of industries, generative AI has become a game-changing tool for improving usefulness and maximizing worker performance. Organizations may greatly increase productivity, teamwork, and decision-making by automating presentation preparation, simplifying communication, and synthesizing meeting findings. This chapter examines the various ways that generative AI can be used to maximize worker performance and usefulness.

8.1 Using AI-Powered Tools to Improve Employee Communication

A key component of any successful organization is effective communication. AI-powered communication solutions may improve teamwork, enable smooth interactions, and guarantee that workers are on the same page with business objectives.

AI-Powered Platforms for Communication:
1. Platforms for communication that allow workers to collaborate effectively from any location can be powered by generative AI. These platforms have the ability to combine many channels such as email, video conferencing, and instant messaging into a single interface.
2. **NLP:** Natural Language Processing AI can comprehend and analyze employee inquiries using natural language processing (NLP), offering pertinent answers or pointing them in the direction of the right resources. This feature improves information flow within teams and reduces communication delays.

Personalized Communication: AI is able to tailor interactions by analyzing the communication preferences and patterns of employees. For instance, it can identify communication styles that work better for particular team members or the optimal times for meetings based on participants' availability.

Personalized Alerts: AI can optimize notifications by comprehending user preferences, guaranteeing that staff members receive important updates without being inundated with unrelated data. This focused strategy aids in sustaining concentration and output.

Enhanced Collaboration:

1. AI technologies, which include features like document sharing, collaborative editing, and project management capabilities, can help to promote real-time collaboration. Workers can collaborate more successfully across regional boundaries.

2. The ability of AI-powered communication platforms to interact with other business tools, such as CRMs and project management software, guarantees that staff members have access to all required resources in a single setting. Overall efficiency is increased and friction is decreased by this integration.

8.2 Using AI to Create Business Presentations

Delivering concepts, plans, and updates requires the

creation of powerful corporate presentations. Creating engaging presentations that successfully convey information to a range of stakeholders can be aided by generative AI.

Automated Slide Generation: AI is able to automatically create slides by analyzing the context and content of a presentation topic. Employees who usually spend hours formatting and arranging presentations can save time by using this approach, which involves choosing suitable templates, layouts, and visuals.

- **Recommended Content:** Based on the presentation topic, generative AI can provide pertinent material, quotes, and visuals. AI can improve the breadth and caliber of presentations by utilizing enormous knowledge databases.

AI algorithms are capable of optimizing visual aspects in presentations, making sure that they follow design principles like image arrangement, text legibility, and color contrast. This focus on detail can greatly increase the presentation's overall impact.

- The visualization of data: Complex data sets can be

converted by generative AI into visually appealing representations like infographics, graphs, and charts that are simple to understand. Stakeholders may swiftly understand important information and make wise decisions with the aid of these visualizations.

AI can help with the creation of tales that are tailored to the tastes and expectations of the audience. AI can suggest changes to tone, vocabulary, and material to optimize engagement by examining prior presentations and audience reaction.

- **Instant Commentary:** Artificial intelligence (AI) solutions can evaluate audience responses during presentations (using engagement metrics and sentiment analysis) and give presenters immediate feedback. With the use of this input, the delivery can be modified to better engage the audience.

8.3 Using AI to Combine Task Insights and Meeting Summaries

Although meetings are essential to organizational operations, they frequently result in a lack of clarity and uncertainty about what has to be done. Generative AI can effectively extract meaningful insights and synthesize meeting outcomes.

Automated Meeting Summaries:
- AI is able to record important points, choices, and action items during meetings by transcribing and summarizing them in real time. Employees are less burdened with taking thorough notes thanks to this automation, which also guarantees that important information is reliably recorded.
- **Highlighting Important Findings:** During meetings, AI algorithms may recognize and highlight important ideas, allowing participants to concentrate on the most pertinent conversations and results.

AI can be used to create, assign, and monitor tasks created during meetings by integrating with task management systems. When an action item is discussed, for example, AI may immediately add it to the appropriate project management application, assign it to the accountable worker, and establish due dates.

- **Reminders for Follow-Up:** AI systems can remind staff members of impending due dates and tasks resulting from meetings, promoting responsibility and on-time work completion.

Ongoing Education and Development:
- AI can offer insights into how to increase the efficacy and efficiency of meetings by examining trends in the conversations and results of those meetings. This could involve suggestions regarding the frequency, length, and tactics for engaging participants in meetings.
- **Loops of Feedback:** By gathering participant opinions on meeting quality and results, AI can help to create feedback loops. Meeting procedures may be continuously improved with the use of this data, keeping them focused and productive.

Organizations have a great chance to maximize employee performance and utility with generative AI. AI enables workers to operate more productively and efficiently by improving communication, simplifying the preparation of presentations, and combining meeting findings. The potential for better teamwork, more informed decision-making, and increased productivity will only increase as more companies use generative AI solutions, setting them up for long-term success in a quickly changing environment.

CHAPTER 9

HEALTHCARE AND SYNTHETIC DATA

In the context of artificial intelligence (AI) and data-driven research, synthetic data has become a game-changing instrument in the healthcare industry. Synthetic data presents a viable substitute for conventional data sources as the need for high-quality data grows. This chapter examines how artificial intelligence (AI) creates synthetic patient data, how it affects clinical research, and the related ethical and privacy concerns.

9.1 AI's Contribution to the Development of Synthetic Patient Data

Artificially created data that closely resembles real patient data without disclosing private information is referred to as synthetic patient data. In order to produce datasets that are statistically representative of real patient populations, artificial intelligence (AI) uses sophisticated algorithms and models.

Generative Adversarial Networks (GANs):

1. **Generative Models:** GANs, one of the most well-known AI methods for producing synthetic data, are made up of two neural networks: a discriminator that assesses the authenticity of the input and a generator that produces new data. The generator creates synthetic datasets that lack identifiable information but maintain key features by learning from actual patient data.

2. **VAEs, or variational autoencoders**: Another technique for creating synthetic data is the employment of VAEs, which learn the distribution of input data and then sample from it to produce new, comparable data points. This method works especially well for producing realistic-looking synthetic patient data that may be applied to a variety of situations.

Data Augmentation: AI can create more synthetic records to supplement current datasets, increasing the volume and diversity of data that can be analyzed. In the healthcare industry, where privacy issues, data scarcity, and legal restrictions can make it difficult to access different patient data, this procedure is essential.

- **Balancing Datasets:** By creating records for underrepresented groups, synthetic data may be used to balance datasets and guarantee that AI models are trained on inclusive and thorough data. Reducing prejudice and increasing the accuracy of healthcare algorithms across various groups depend on this balancing.

Testing and Validation:
- Synthetic data must be validated to make sure it faithfully captures the underlying patterns and correlations seen in actual patient data before it can be used in clinical or research settings. By measuring the similarities and differences between synthetic and real data, artificial intelligence (AI) approaches can assist in evaluating the accuracy of synthetic datasets.
- The process of iterative refinement Iterative processes are frequently used to create synthetic data, with models being continuously improved in

response to user feedback and performance indicators. The generated synthetic data is kept current and valuable for clinical and research applications thanks to this ongoing process.

9.2 How Clinical Research Is Accelerated by Synthetic Data

Clinical research could undergo a revolution thanks to synthetic data, which can solve a number of issues with speed, quality, and access to data. Research procedures are made more effective by synthetic data, which offers high-quality, easily accessible datasets.

Enhanced Data Availability:
- By removing obstacles to data access, synthetic data enables researchers to work with big datasets without requiring the kind of lengthy ethical approvals and permissions that are usually required for real patient data. This accessibility speeds up research timelines, allowing for quicker testing of hypotheses and investigation of novel medical questions.

- **Interdepartmental Cooperation:** Researchers don't have to worry about patient privacy or data breaches when sharing synthetic datasets between universities. This partnership promotes creative solutions to healthcare problems and expands our collective knowledge.

Sped up Drug Development:
- Synthetic data can greatly expedite the process of identifying possible clinical trial candidates in medication development. Before actual testing starts, researchers can assess the safety and effectiveness of medications by modeling patient reactions to different treatments.
- **Modeling for Prediction:** Researchers can create and evaluate prediction models that can predict therapeutic efficacy, side effects, and patient outcomes using synthetic datasets. These models have the potential to improve trial designs and direct decision-making procedures, which will ultimately result in better clinical outcomes.

Cost Efficiency:

- Clinical research expenses can be decreased by using synthetic data. Healthcare organizations can more efficiently deploy resources and concentrate on research projects that spur innovation by reducing the need for intensive patient recruiting and data administration.
- **Reduction in Time to Market:** Synthetic data can improve patient care and optimize resource allocation by reducing the time needed to introduce innovative therapies and interventions to the market through faster data availability and better predictive modeling.

9.3 Consequences for Privacy and the Moral Application of Synthetic Data

Although there are many benefits to using synthetic data, there are also significant privacy and ethical issues that need to be resolved to guarantee responsible use in the medical field.

Protection of Data Privacy:
- The capacity of synthetic data to preserve patient

privacy is among its most important advantages. Synthetic datasets allow for study without jeopardizing individual privacy by producing data devoid of identifiable information. To guarantee that synthetic data cannot be re-identified or connected to actual patients, strict protections must be put in place.

- **Compliance with Regulations:** It is imperative for healthcare institutions to make sure that their use of synthetic data conforms with current standards, including the United States' Health Insurance Portability and Accountability Act (HIPAA). Clear rules for the moral application of synthetic data must be established in order to preserve patient rights and public confidence.

Ethical Issues in the Creation of Data:

- Ethical guidelines must be followed while creating synthetic data to prevent the data from reinforcing prejudices or misrepresenting demographics. Because biased training data might result in skewed synthetic datasets, researchers need to be careful about the data sources they utilize to train generative models.

- **Accountability and Transparency:** Businesses that use synthetic data should be open and honest about the methods they use and how they generate their data. Accountability is encouraged by this transparency, which also makes it possible for stakeholders to comprehend the creation and application of synthetic data in research.

Keeping Innovation and Responsibility in Check:
- The growing use of synthetic data in healthcare necessitates striking a balance between fostering innovation and upholding moral accountability. In order to traverse the complexity of using synthetic data, stakeholders need to have constant conversations. This will encourage cooperation between researchers, ethicists, and policymakers in order to create best practices and recommendations.

By improving data accessibility, speeding up clinical research, and resolving privacy issues, synthetic data has the potential to completely transform the healthcare industry. The healthcare industry can get over long-standing obstacles related to data access and quality by creatively using AI to create fake patient data. However, to guarantee that the advantages of synthetic data are achieved responsibly and fairly, it is imperative to maintain vigilance about privacy issues and ethical considerations. The appropriate use of synthetic data will be essential to fostering innovation and enhancing patient outcomes as the healthcare industry develops further.

CHAPTER 10

GENERATIVE AI'S ROLE IN BUSINESS

Generative AI has the potential to completely transform the business environment in a number of industries as we approach the dawn of a new technology era. Its uses range from strategic planning to advertising, changing how businesses function and compete in a world that is becoming more and more digital. The future of generative AI in business is explored in this chapter, with particular attention paid to its application in advertising, global company strategy, and the long-term effects on worker productivity.

10.1 AI in Advertising: AI Ad Models from Google and Meta

The advertising industry has seen a huge transformation thanks to generative AI, which enables businesses to develop more individualized, successful, and efficient advertising campaigns. Google and Meta (previously Facebook), two significant organizations, have led the way in incorporating AI into their advertising strategies by utilizing generative technology to improve user engagement and increase conversions.

Personalization at Scale:
- By evaluating enormous volumes of data, such as browsing history, demographics, and preferences, generative AI allows advertisers to present customers with highly customized content. With the help of this feature, companies may produce customized ad experiences that appeal to certain users and raise engagement rates.
- To ensure that the ads displayed are timely and relevant, Google's AI models, for instance, can create personalized ad copy depending on user behavior and search queries. In a similar vein, Meta generates dynamic advertisements using generative algorithms that modify content in response to user interactions in real time.

Creative Automation:

- By automating the creative process, generative AI enables marketers to swiftly create a variety of ad content variations. This automation preserves a high level of quality while cutting down on the time and resources needed to create content.
- AI-powered tools can produce images, short videos, and even music, giving marketers access to a wealth of creative resources. In addition to streamlining the process, this gives marketers the ability to do A/B testing more successfully and optimize campaigns based on real-time input.

Enhanced Targeting and Attribution:
- AI-powered advertising models use predictive analytics to find potential clients, improving targeting accuracy. Businesses may more efficiently distribute their advertising money and make sure that their messages are seen by the appropriate people at the right time by examining past data and user behavior trends.
- Furthermore, by evaluating the effectiveness of different touchpoints in a customer's journey, generative AI improves attribution models.

Marketers may use this all-inclusive perspective to identify the ads that are generating conversions and adjust their approach accordingly.

10.2 Generative AI's Place in International Business Strategy

Generative AI is essential in helping companies shape their strategic ambitions as they traverse a global marketplace that is becoming more linked and competitive. Its capacity to evaluate information, forecast patterns, and produce insights enables businesses to take well-informed decisions and promote long-term success.

Data-Driven Decision Making:
- By evaluating huge datasets and producing useful insights, generative AI helps with data-driven decision-making. Companies can use these data to predict market trends, comprehend consumer preferences, and find market possibilities.
- AI models, for example, may evaluate customer sentiment across geographies, assisting businesses in customizing their approaches to suit regional tastes

and cultural quirks. Customer satisfaction and market penetration are improved by this localized strategy.

Simulation and Scenario Planning:
- Organizations can perform scenario planning by using generative AI to simulate different business scenarios and outcomes. Leaders are able to assess possible strategies and their effects on market dynamics, risk, and performance thanks to this competence.
- Businesses can use AI to develop virtual models that forecast the results of various strategic decisions, including new product introductions or market expansions. Organizations can better plan for unforeseen circumstances and make well-informed decisions that support their long-term objectives by visualizing possible outcomes.

Innovation and Agility:
- Agility is critical in a company environment that is changing quickly. By allowing businesses to test out novel concepts, goods, and services without being

constrained by conventional procedures, generative AI promotes innovation. Companies may use AI to swiftly prototype ideas and gain input from target audiences, which enables them to iterate and launch creative solutions ahead of rivals. In addition to improving competitive advantage, this agility fosters an innovative culture within businesses.

10.3 Generative AI's Long-Term Effect on Workforce Productivity

Workforce productivity is expected to be significantly impacted by the incorporation of generative AI into corporate operations. Generative AI creates a more productive workplace by automating repetitive chores and enhancing human abilities, freeing up staff members to concentrate on higher-value work.

Task Automation:
- Generative AI is excellent at automating routine and repetitive work, freeing up staff members to focus on strategic projects that call for imagination and critical thinking. AI may manage data entry, report

production, and simple consumer inquiries, for example, freeing up human personnel to work on more difficult problem-solving assignments. This change not only increases output but also lowers the possibility of human mistake that comes with manual procedures, producing more precise results and increased operational effectiveness.

The term "augmented intelligence" refers to Generative artificial intelligence is an augmentative technology that improves productivity and decision-making rather than taking the place of human labor. Workers are able to make better, faster decisions by using AI-generated insights to guide their strategy.

- AI, for instance, can evaluate patient data to find possible health hazards, enabling medical professionals to treat patients proactively. AI in finance can help analysts better understand market trends, which will improve investment plans and results.

The process of reskilling and upskilling: Organizations are investing in reskilling and upskilling their personnel as a result of the need for a shift in workforce skills brought about by the advent of generative AI. Employees will need to develop new skills to meet the changing needs of the workplace as regular tasks become automated. Businesses that put a high priority on training programs can develop a workforce that is more flexible and capable of utilizing AI technologies efficiently. In addition to improving employee engagement and pleasure, this emphasis on ongoing learning fortifies organizational resilience against technological upheaval.

Generative AI has a bright future in business, with the potential to revolutionize global strategy, labor productivity, and advertising. As businesses continue to use AI, they will open up new avenues for creativity, productivity, and expansion. But using generative AI also necessitates a careful strategy to handle moral issues and guarantee that the advantages of this technology are used sensibly. Businesses may take the lead in the generative AI revolution and make a long-lasting difference in the global marketplace by finding this equilibrium.

ABOUT THE AUTHOR

Renowned business strategist, author, and consultant James Royce Smartman has over twenty years of experience in a variety of fields, including corporate management, entrepreneurship, and finance. James has a strong academic background and an MBA from a prestigious university. As a result, he has a good understanding of the nuances of contemporary business practices and market dynamics.

James has held executive positions in multiple Fortune 500 businesses over his career, effectively leading projects that have sparked efficiency, growth, and innovation. Because of his special combination of theoretical knowledge and real-world experience, he can offer organizations of all sizes frameworks and concrete tactics.

James is regularly asked to speak at conferences and seminars as a thought leader in the business sector, offering his knowledge on subjects including strategic planning, organizational behavior, and leadership development. In

ACKNOWLEDGMENTS

My sincere appreciation goes out to everyone who helped to make this book possible.

This book is based on the work of the pioneers of artificial intelligence and the creative minds that never stop pushing the boundaries of what is possible.

To my coworkers, mentors, and business leaders who contributed their knowledge, opinions, and experiences, your advice and assistance have been crucial during this process.

Thank you to my family and friends for your everlasting support and understanding; your faith in me has always inspired me.

Lastly, I would like to thank the readers for their curiosity and enthusiasm for learning. I hope this book encourages you to investigate AI's revolutionary possibilities and confidently face the future.

Without all of you, this job would not have been possible. Thank you.

addition, he frequently contributes his thoughts on new trends and best practices to eminent business journals.

James Royce Smartman is devoted to helping company executives and entrepreneurs realize their objectives by providing them with creative solutions and useful guidance. His writings seek to demystify difficult business ideas so that readers of all skill levels can understand and use them. James offers a road map for success that is in line with the changing business environment of today by emphasizing practical examples and tried-and-true tactics.

James regularly mentors young professionals and supports different business projects that foster entrepreneurship and innovation in addition to his writing and consulting work. He promotes an organizational culture that welcomes change and encourages expansion because he believes in the value of teamwork and ongoing education.

www.ingramcontent.com/pod-product-compliance
Lightning Source LLC
Chambersburg PA
CBHW050316230526
4547ICB00005B/2213